A Graceful Age

A Graceful Age

Reflections for the Wisdom Years

Mark LaMont, FSC

Saint Mary's Press
Christian Brothers Publications
Winona, Minnesota

The publishing team included Michael Wilt, development editor; Laurie A. Berg, copy editor; James H. Gurley, production editor; Hollace Storkel, typesetter; Cindi Ramm, cover designer; pre-press, printing, and binding by the graphics division of Saint Mary's Press.

Printed in the United States of America

Printing: 9 8 7 6 5 4 3 2 1

Year: 2007 06 05 04 03 02 01 00 99

ISBN 0-88489-617-X

Genuine recycled paper with 10% post-consumer waste. Printed with soy-based ink.

This book is dedicated to the elderly, who teach us fortitude and patience in their trials and sufferings, courtesy and empathy in their service to their peers, and faith and hope as they look to the future.

Contents

Introduction

Those who have had any significant contact with the elderly, whether they had contact as a relative, a friend, a social worker, or a volunteer, will agree that those who have been blessed with length of years will experience certain losses. These losses for the most part occur within a short period of time: the loss of one's spouse, friends, home, health, and independence. Any experienced loss is inevitably associated with pain, which is followed by some reaction to it. These reactions can be physical, psychological, spiritual, or a combination of all three.

To relieve the pain caused by a particular loss, people may take drugs, may become depressed, or may turn to the religious aspects of their life for comfort and understanding. It is to those who choose the spiritual option that this book is directed.

Most of the prayers presented here were suggested by persons in nursing homes, in high rises, in private homes, or at senior-citizen centers. To these suggestions I have added other topics based on my own needs and experiences.

The various reflections offer a minicourse on theology, combined with appropriate prayer. As one reads any given reflection, the content will probably call to mind the first time these instructions or directives were heard. Such reminiscing is good for the soul. It can be a source of hope and consolation, affirming that one has practiced a given virtue or maintained a good habit for most of a lifetime. The reflections will also provide an opportunity for one to renew the practice of some spiritual exercise that has been neglected for a while, which in turn will provide a boost to one's present prayer life.

Although these reflections are intended for private prayer, it is not out of the question that these exercises could be used as a basis for faith sharing in a prayer group. Readers may choose to follow the order of the book, reading one reflection per day, or to skip around, choosing meditations of particular interest at a particular time. If a special need arises in one's life, the reader would do well to scan the table of contents for a theme that might be especially appropriate in that time of need.

A Message to the Younger Generations

An estimated twenty-five million people in the United States are classified as elderly. If the same percentage holds true throughout the world, the number would be over a billion. Those of you in younger age-groups must be congratulated for the care, respect, and services you give to help ease the pain, losses, and loneliness of senior citizens. You may on special occasions wish to show your affection for a beloved elder in your life. Gifts of clothes, flowers, candy, and so on, while sometimes useful and appropriate, can at times seem trite and redundant. This book offers a meaningful and lasting alternative.

Aging 1

Do not reject me in my old age,
nor desert me when my strength is failing. . . .
Now that I am old and grey-haired,
God, do not desert me.

—Psalm 71:9,18

Old age is like climbing a mountain. The higher you get, the more tired and breathless you become. But your view becomes much more extensive.

—Ingmar Bergman

Growing old has one advantage: you'll never have to do it again.

—Anonymous

First you are young; then you are middle-aged; then you are old; then you are wonderful.

—Anonymous

Becoming or being old is not a mystery. At our first birthday, our parents said simply, "My child is one year old." But we've all known people who seem old at forty and others who do not seem old at eighty. Psychologists say that so-called aging has to do with our self-image, how we relate to relatives and friends, how we view God, and our attitude toward life and death.

The key word here is *attitude,* for our attitude is behind the way we think, feel, and act—and what we say and do determines how others know us. Not much explanation is needed—this is the way we see ourselves and want others to see us.

Our self-image has a lot to do with our relations with close family members and friends; they see us as we are and treat us accordingly, and we reciprocate.

When we consider attitude, we should consider our own—and not the attitude of younger generations toward us. However, we would be less than truthful if we refused to admit that some aspects of aging are the pits. But in certain areas we can be the best we have ever been—in wisdom, patience, compassion, judgment, know-how, and tolerance, just to mention a few. All things considered, growing old is not negative as long as our attitude toward life does not sour. The beauty of life is that we are in control of our thoughts, our attitudes. We can think of ourselves not as old but as just more experienced.

Age is a quality of mind.
If you have left your dreams behind,
If hope is cold, if you no longer look ahead,
If your ambitions' fires are dead—
Then you are old.
But if from life you take the best,
And if in life you keep the jest,
If love you hold;
No matter how the birthdays fly,
You are not old.

—Anonymous

Prayer

God, although aging is a natural process that all must face, it is difficult to admit that I am not as young as I was. It is not so much being old that is difficult to bear—not the wrinkles, the graying, the false teeth, the loss of hearing and sight—rather it's feeling out-of-date and unimportant that is the agony. When I was young, I had energy to burn as I tried to make a mark in the world. But as I grow old, I am forced to sit quietly by and watch others redo what I have done, or erase it altogether. Give me wisdom in my growing old, God, and the knowledge that I have done what I could, so I can smile in peace as others take their turn in the game of life. Amen.

Aging 2

Old age and know-how will overcome youth and skill.

—Anonymous

Who well lives, long lives; for this age of ours,
Should not be numbered by years, days, and hours.

—Seigneur Du Bartas

Because life expectancies are longer now than in the past, the subject of ageism has been discussed with greater frequency. Ageism is the practice of a systematic stereotyping, or a discrimination based on age—a belief that people are competent human beings only between the ages of eighteen and sixty-five. Like any other prejudice, ageism is detrimental to both those who hold that prejudice and those who suffer from it.

Recent studies show that the older people become, the more they differ from one another. The only true generalization possible about age is that no generalization is possible.

A recent poll shows that nearly two-thirds of those who are age sixty-five and over are happy with their lives. Only half of those between the ages of eighteen and forty-nine are happy. Age clearly has something going for it.

One of the advantages of being older is the increased freedom that is enjoyed. A person can set his or her goals and the pace to achieve them. There is time to pursue hobbies and other interests.

Later years can also bring exciting opportunities, such as a second career, volunteer work, tutoring, involvement with senior centers, and further education. Many have broadened their horizons by participating in elder hostel programs both here and abroad.

Performing activities to our liking makes a person feel alive and vibrant. It means one still has a role to play in the drama of life, and that one is still needed.

Prayer

My God, I thank you for the days of my life. I thank you for the chance to rise when I have fallen, to simplify the complexities of my past, to advance in wisdom and age and grace. I am delighted with my present, marked by silver-gray and the infirmities of advancing years. I rejoice in your love, in the love of my relatives and friends, and in the youthful daily challenge to grow in that love. Make my heart sing as you lead me into your final loving embrace. Amen.

Angels

It was an angel speaking to him.

—John 12:29

The servants of Christ are protected by invisible, rather than visible, beings. But if these guard you, they do so because they have been summoned by your prayer.

—Saint Ambrose

If you find it impossible to pray, charge your Good Angel to pray in your stead.

—Saint John Vianney

Some people have entertained angels without knowing it.

—Hebrews 13:2

Belief in guardian angels is a long-standing aspect of the Christian faith. Guardian angels perform four services for each of us. They are protectors. They keep us from physical, mental, and spiritual harm. They are rescuers. When we have encountered some danger and have experienced an injury, they assist in the healing process. They are communicators, who tell us what God wants us to do or not do in the events and decisions of our life. And guardian angels are intercessors. They constantly ask God for the graces we need to lead a good life and to succeed in our endeavors.

My angel knows me inside and out, and loves me just the way I am. My angel speaks to me in many different ways; it is my duty to listen. My guardian angel helps me find a place when I feel I have no place to go. When I feel lonely, my angel makes suggestions to keep me busy and in the service of others.

Prayer

Angel Guardian, I thank you for the protection and guidance you have provided during my life. I especially remember times when you saved me from serious illness or injury, and times when you helped me make decisions that changed my life. I ask for your inspiration every day of my life and at the hour of my death. Amen.

Art

We are God's work of art.

—Ephesians 2:10

Art proceeds from a spontaneous instinct like love
does; it must be cultivated like friendship.

—Raisa Maritain

Every artist may not be a special kind of person. But
every person is a special kind of artist.

—Eric Gill

The arts are universal. No people on earth
have done without the arts, from the earliest paintings on cave walls and the theatrical
depictions of important events in tribal life,
to the works in modern museums, Broadway
shows, and grand opera.

Works of art prepare us for action. This
action is far reaching—the goals of art coincide with the goals of life. Art, though often
looked on as a means of getting out of the
hustle and bustle of the boring side of our life,

is in reality a person's way of acting in the world. Art is a necessity.

What would our world be without the musician, the poet, the dramatist, the sculptor, the architect! It is difficult to imagine our existence without them. How many concerts, plays, and art exhibits have you enjoyed during your lifetime, not to mention the music, plays, and visuals you have experienced through radio and television? They have all played a part in your life as an individual and as a person in friendship and community.

But let us not forget the most perfect works of art created by the Divine Artist: the persons in our life, and all of nature.

Prayer

Glory and praise be to you, Divine Artist, for all the beautiful things you have created for my enjoyment, education, and spiritual growth. May I continue to receive the workings of your Spirit for my welfare and that of others. Amen.

Charity

Where there is charity and wisdom, there is neither fear nor ignorance. Where there is patience and humility, there is neither anger nor vexation.

—Saint Francis of Assisi

God is love, and whoever remains in love remains in God.

—1 John 4:16

[What matters is] faith working through love.

—Galatians 5:6

The virtue of charity (love) has been used in so many ways in our relations with persons, places, and things that it is sometimes difficult to define it or to understand it in our life situations. We do not love things in the same way or degree that we love people, and the events of our life are not cherished in the same way that people and things are. It may be of help to associate charity with two other virtues: faith and humility.

Many elements of our religious upbringing are difficult to understand. One of these is how people relate to one another. To improve our relationships, we must have the faith to believe that the majority of the people we know—and those we don't know—are basically good persons. God is more caring and loving, and less stringent, than we are in our judgment and criticism of others.

Every sort of love is marked by humility. When we love people, we think that they are worth more than we are. Isn't that what is missing when we fail to listen to the ones with whom we have the closest ties? Believe it or not, the Creator of the universe is most accurately revealed to us as the man on his knees, washing the feet of his disciples, associating with sinners, and accepting the disappointments he experienced even among his Apostles and his friends.

Its takes humility to admit that we have made a mistake and to apologize for our actions. And it takes humility to accept an apology from another and to say, "You are forgiven." When you humble yourself before another, it is a sure sign of trust and love. One who apologizes sincerely rarely goes unforgiven.

Prayer

God, I hold quietly in my mind the names of the persons I find it difficult to love: those of whom I am afraid, jealous, or envious, or those who may have done harm to me at some point in my life. I pray that your good will may be done for them and for me. Grant us forgiveness and love. Amen.

The Church

You are Peter and on this rock I will build my community. And the gates of the underworld can never overpower it.

—Matthew 16:18

Nothing lasts but the church.

—George Herbert

The word *church* has many different meanings and implications. When a person says, "I am going to church," he or she may be speaking of visiting the church to admire its architectural structure, of going to pray, of joining others in some religious service, or of simply enjoying some peace and quiet. Some people never go to church—that is, they never enter a physical structure for purposes like those just mentioned. This does not mean, however, that they never participate in "church" activities. They may choose, for example, to practice their religion in a less formal manner or in more natural surroundings or through participation in arts such as painting and dance.

Why do I belong to a particular church or religion—Jewish, Muslim, Christian, or any other? My particular membership probably resulted from the influence of my parents, environment, upbringing, teachers, and personal experiences and encounters.

What do I expect from my church? These are my primary expectations:

- authority and leadership in my search for truth
- encouragement and support in making decisions
- faith and hope for a better life, here and hereafter
- love, empathy, and forgiveness when I fail

Throughout history my church has baffled me with its infighting and divisive goings-on, but I still love my church for what it represents. I have witnessed scandal in my church, yet it has made me understand holiness. My church seemed to have been destroyed, or to have destroyed itself, but it is still present. My church has been obscure, compromised, false, and detested, but I also find it holy, generous, humble, and beautiful.

For a variety of reasons, some have left what was once their church. I have no choice but to remain with mine because I believe I am church. Where I am is church.

Prayer

God, I thank you for the church to which you have called me to be a member. May the members support one another and be of service to others. Amen.

The Commandments

The law and the commandment . . . I have written
for their instruction.

—Exodus 24:12

If you desire wisdom, keep the commandments.

—Sirach 1:26

In vain we call old notions fudge,
And bend our conscience to our dealing;
The Ten Commandments will not budge,
And stealing *will* continue stealing.

—James Russell Lowell

R egulations, precepts, directions, customs,
practices, right conduct, legalism, ethics,
morals, civil law, church law, divine law, natural law—these terms ring in our ears throughout our life. So many attempts are made to
keep people from going astray that it is almost
impossible to know every prohibition that
exists. It has been said that the government
adds hundreds of new laws each year to the
ridiculously long list that already exists (many

of which, by the way, can no longer be applied or sanctioned!). We cannot help but be overwhelmed.

But do not lose heart. God is not as demanding as humans are. God gave us just ten commandments, and God's Son, Jesus, reduced these to two.

Knowing all the laws of the entire world will not make us better people. A firm belief in the "why" of a law, and knowing that why we should or should not act is based on the motive of love, will help us live as God intended us to live—in the image of God.

The best laws are intended to educate, instruct, and make us holy. How we observe the Commandments is the basis of our morality, which is concerned with three things: the relations between persons, the motives of each person, and the relations of each person with God.

Prayer

My prayer today is one of confidence that God will give me faith and motivation to observe God's laws so that I may live according to God's will and in harmony with all people. Amen.

Creation

God saw all he had made, and indeed it was very good.
>   —Genesis 1:31

To act is to create, and creation is forever.
>   —Teilhard de Chardin

If I had to define life in a word, it would be: Life is creation.
>   —Claude Bernard

Everything is good when it leaves the hands of the Creator; everything degenerates in the hands of man.
>   —Jean Jacques Rousseau

When we take time to think of the marvelous universe that God has created, we are overwhelmed. Each day new discoveries are made on earth and in the heavens. No single person can know fully the flora and fauna of the world. Think for a moment of the various species of insects in the world. Our experience is probably limited to flies, mosquitoes, ticks, spiders, bees, butterflies, and termites, but these creatures barely scratch the surface when it comes to the total number of species in existence. God created all things for our service and our good, and for us to care for, even though we do not always understand God's plan or reason.

Although we have this marvelous universe before us, it seems clear from experience and reflection that the work of creation is never complete. Humans were created to be God's coworkers in the work of creation. This task will continue to the end of time.

It may be difficult to picture yourself in the role of creator, but reflecting on your past will show that you have brought into being persons and things that have made this world a better and brighter place. God has chosen you to bring life into the world through your children. If you do not have offspring, your relatives, friends, and acquaintances have become new individuals because you have been a part of their lives. Any time you help others—talk to them in their grief, comfort them in their loss, laugh with them, volunteer your services—you are a creator.

God gives other creative gifts and talents as well: painting and drawing, writing, sculpting, landscaping, gardening, and so on. From the building of Noah's ark and the Tower of Babel to the making of the most technologically advanced structures in the world, humans cocreate with God.

Sometimes we may be negative and cynical about creation, as Rousseau was in the preceding quotation. The blemishes on creation—pollution, slums, starvation, violent conflicts among nations—have the potential to make us cynical, even cause us to despair. But on the positive side, humans have the creative powers to eliminate these blemishes. May we celebrate and use our creative powers.

Prayer

God, I thank you for the gifts and talents you have bestowed on me to be a creator with you. Grant me a special grace to use them for your honor and glory and to make this a better world. Thank you for the days when I feel like making history, like creating a new world. I believe that I am history. I create what I am. I am a reflection of you and of creation. Amen.

The Cross

If anyone wants to be a follower of mine, let him
renounce himself and take up his cross and follow me.
—Matthew 16:24

The way of bliss lies not on beds of down,
And he that has no cross deserves no crown.
—Francis Quarles

Often the test of courage is to live.
Anyone can die.
—Vittorio Alfieri

The trials and crosses we witness and experience in life are often beyond comprehen-
sion. These crosses come in many forms and
encompass the entire range of living: physical,
emotional, spiritual. It is probably safe to say
that every person on earth has endured crosses
in all three areas. We all have physical crosses
to bear—illness, injury, aging—some more
prolonged than others. Fears, worries, and
anxieties concerning the past, present, and
future are our emotional crosses. Our spiritual

crosses come at periods when we wish to pray but can't, when we feel obligated to pray but don't want to, or when we feel that our prayer is not effective—as well as at times when God seems distant or nonexistent or worthy of nothing but our anger.

Some of these crosses seem heavier than others and have to be endured for a longer time. But every cross is an essential part of living and necessary for growing, for becoming a better person. No human being can get through life without carrying some cross. This is especially true for Christians.

We need to cultivate three virtues if we are to endure the crosses of life: hope, patience, and courage. *Hope* that the cross will pass, but not before we are improved by it; *patience* to accept the cross and to endure it as long as it lasts; and *courage* to persevere and to resist defeat. With these three virtues, crosses will mean growth in the midst of setbacks.

Prayer

God, I accept the crosses of my life, by which the world is crucified to me and I to the world.

Grant me the gifts of hope, patience, and courage so that I may profit by the crosses that will come to me during life. Amen.

Death and Dying 1

On their dying day they will be blessed.
—Sirach 1:13

We are all equal in the presence of death.
—Publilius Syrus

When you were born you cried
And the whole world rejoiced.
Live in such a way that when you die
The whole world cries and you rejoice.
—Traditional Indian saying

Call no one fortunate before his death;
It is by his end that someone will be known.
—Sirach 11:28

It seems that very few of us know how to die. Dying, like living, is an art. If we sought to learn as much about how to die as we do about how to live, many more people would die happy. The truth is that the art of living does not differ from the art of dying. We learn how to die by learning how to live.

As I think of dying, I am automatically overcome by fear and anxiety. A sure way of conquering fear is to honestly and humbly admit, "I am afraid." A good practice is to find a quiet spot where you can be alone. Make yourself comfortable, let your mind become quiet, and repeat words such as these:

I admit that I am afraid of dying. I am not going to pretend anymore. I am going to face my fear as the first step to overcoming it.

What are some of the fears we need to conquer? According to John Whitehead in his book *A Practical Guide to Death and Dying*, we fear one or all of the following:
- pain and physical suffering
- loss, both in terms of separation from loved ones and friends and loss of our faculties
- the meaninglessness that comes with the feeling of not being needed or loved, or of being a failure
- the unknown; that is, we cannot know in advance the nature of the afterlife
- nonbeing, the total disappearance of one's identity

Our training and education tell us that these fears can be overcome through learning, judgment, and reasoning. However, the fear of death is not rational—it is very emotional, and emotions are not easily controlled or changed by logic. Hence, it seems necessary to face the fears one by one, admitting that each fear is a part of oneself.

Despite the fear of dying, we have confidence that on our journey to the unknown, we have the support we will need. We know it is a communal journey, a communal pilgrimage to some Holy City.

Prayer

Heavenly and gracious God, free me from the deceptive fear of dying. Give me the assurance that my life on earth may be a preamble to life eternal. Amen.

Death and Dying 2

Death is swallowed up in victory. Death, where is
your victory? Death, where is your sting?
—1 Corinthians 15:54–55

For God did not make Death,
he takes no pleasure in destroying the living.
—Wisdom 1:13

As for me, if I lie down and sleep, I shall awake.
—Psalm 3:5

Cowards die many times before their deaths;
The valiant never taste of death but once.
Of all the wonders that I yet have heard,
It seems to me most strange that men should fear;
Seeing that death, a necessary end,
Will come when it will come.
—William Shakespeare

There is something beyond the grave; death does not
end all.
—Sextus Propertius

There is a difference between death and dying. The first is a biological process, a function of the body. The latter is a psychological process, a function of the mind. Death, by nature, is the biological process inherent in every living being. As Ecclesiastes says, "There is a season for everything. . . . a time for giving birth, a time for dying" (3:1–2).

Only humans are afraid to die. Other animals go to their death without fear. This is not contrary to the fact that they struggle to live— the bear flees the hunter, the deer hides from the wolf, the bird tries to avoid the snare. But these actions are done by instinct. Unlike humans, animals do not have a sense of time by which they can anticipate their death. Unlike humans, animals do not have a sense of self-worth that can be projected into the future. Unlike humans, animals do not reason that they may be immortal.

One of the basic human instincts is to seek immortality. This manifests itself when we seek fame, fortune, status, titles, possessions, power. It is seen in our monuments of steel and stone that strive to make us permanent, hence immortal. At the same time, these are evidence of our denial of death.

It is necessary for our peace of mind that we realistically accept that we are mortal. Death belongs to life, as does birth. Because of our gifts of intelligence and reasoning, we alone know that we are finite, but also destined for a future life.

Prayer

God, grant me the special grace to overcome my fear of dying, and the courage to face death with faith and hope in the future. Amen.

Death
and the Afterlife

I am the resurrection,
Anyone who believes in me, even though that person
    dies, will live,
and whoever lives and believes in me
will never die.

—John 11:25–26

Have I not told you that if you believe you will see
the glory of God?

—John 11:40

In truth I tell you, today you will be with me in paradise.

—Luke 23:43

God created human beings to be immortal,
He made them as an image of his own nature.

—Wisdom 2:23

Death be not proud, though some have called thee
Mighty and dreadful, for thou art not so,
For those whom thou think'st thou dost overthrow,
Die not, poor death, nor yet canst thou kill me.

—John Donne

Throughout history, people from all levels of society—religious and civil leaders, teachers, poets, workers—have arrived at the conclusion that there is life after death. Some have arrived at this conviction by way of logic, some by accepting the teaching of others. Most, however, come to this conviction by way of faith and hope that the divinity of humans never perishes.

In our inmost being, we all long for eternal life. It is unthinkable to imagine that one's father, mother, husband, wife, child, or friend will just disappear without a trace and be no more. It is unbearable to think that everything we have accomplished will be lost forever, or that we, on whom so much labor, sacrifice, blood, and sweat has been spent, will simply vanish.

"I live and you also will live," Jesus told his disciples (John 14:19). God created the world for life, not for death. God was present at our birth, remains with us on our earthly journey, and will greet us in eternity. God is the First and the Last, the Beginning and the End, the Alpha and the Omega. Jesus sometimes spoke of eternal life in terms of resurrection, and in the Christian creed we say, "We believe in the resurrection of the body." Life after death is a firm conviction of Christian faith.

In hope and faith, let us consider the following thoughts by an anonymous author, found in a Carmelite monastery in Ireland and often used as a reflection at memorial services:

"Together"

Death is nothing at all.
I have only slipped away into the next room.
Whatever we were to each other, we are still.
Call me by my old familiar name,
speak to me in the easy way you always did.
It is the same as it always was;
there is absolutely unbroken continuity.
Why should I be out of your mind
because I am out of your sight?
I am waiting for you somewhere very near.
Nothing is past, nothing is lost.
One brief moment and it will be as it was
    before,
only better, infinitely happier and forever;
we will be together in Christ.

Prayer

God, I pray in the words of John Cardinal Newman:

Support us all the day long of this troublesome life, until the shadows lengthen, and the evening comes, and the busy world is hushed, and the fever of life is over, and our work is done. Then in your mercy grant us a safe lodging, and a holy rest, and peace at last. Through Jesus our Lord. Amen.

Faith

Your faith has saved you.

—Matthew 9:22

And if you have faith, everything you ask for in prayer, you will receive.

—Matthew 21:22

Blessed are those who have not seen and yet believe.

—John 20:29

It would be interesting to know how many generations ago, within my family, the passing on of the faith I now profess was started. I sometimes wonder about my ancestors, who first accepted the faith and passed it on from one generation to the next until my parents handed it on to me. Others perhaps did not receive faith in this manner. Perhaps they received their faith from the example of a person far removed from their family tree. Whatever the source, we must remember that faith is a gift.

We would not be what we are today were it not for the faith we were given and the grace that preserves it throughout a lifetime.

Someone once defined faith as an illogical belief in the occurrence of the improbable. Faith often seems opposed to logic and reason. In the modern world, when technological advances seem to give many people the power to accomplish the improbable, it is no wonder that faith seems to get pushed to the background. But let us remember, to paraphrase Oliver Wendell Holmes, that the great act of faith is when a person decides that he or she is not God.

Prayer

God, I thank you for the gift of my faith. With the father of the demoniac son I pray: "I have faith. Help my lack of faith!" (Mark 9:24). Amen.

Faith and Works

Faith without deeds is useless.

—James 2:20

In all truth I tell you,
whoever believes in me
will perform the same works as I do myself.

—John 14:12

We say we have faith, but we fail to open our purses to the poor. We claim faith, but we don't empathize with the immigrant. We believe, we say, but we don't contribute to the food shelf. We have great beliefs, but we do not come to the relief of a neighbor. And who is my neighbor? Not just the person next door or down the street but anyone who needs my help, whether in this country or across the oceans.

When Christ said that the believer will do the same works that he does, Christ was not referring just to miracles but to any work or act in which we are involved to help lessen the burdens of others.

People of faith are people of the Beatitudes. They are the generous volunteers of the world. They expect no pay or reward. They see a need, take the time and energy, and pitch in to help complete the task at hand. They are the people who live in love, act in the name of truth, and honor life. Those who are no longer physically able to assist others still have a volunteer service to perform: prayer. They have a special place in their prayers for the end of the misfortunes in the world.

Prayer

God, give me a generous heart to listen to the persons who need my help, and grace to put my faith into action. At times when I cannot physically assist, receive the prayers I offer for the relief of those who are suffering. I offer this prayer in the name of Jesus. Amen.

God

For it is I . . . who am your God.

—Leviticus 11:44

What sort of God would it be,
who only pushes from without?

—Goethe

It is in [God] that we live, and move, and exist.

—Acts of the Apostles 17:28

Who is God? Who is your God? It seems that everyone wants to know who God is. We are all seeking something that is often called God. We are less than human without this hunger for God.

Many theologians claim that God alone is our fulfillment. That may be true, but the majority of us are not theologians, and asking us to believe that God alone is our fulfillment is asking a lot of us.

It is doubtful that any two persons have the same idea of God, even if they were brought up in the same religion, have similar backgrounds and associations, and have like educations and experiences. On the other hand, a Hindu, a Jew, a Muslim, and a Christian may have the same God. This fact alone should encourage religious tolerance.

Belief in God and in the images used to help understand God are related to the rituals and metaphors we use, as well as to the people in our life, the environment in which we find ourselves, and our experiences. Rituals are found everywhere: they can involve candles, incense, dance, art, music, and so on. Metaphors are used to explain difficult concepts by suggesting a likeness between two things, such as seeing God as Father, Mother, First and Last, Love, Lifegiver, or Wisdom. The many metaphors used in reference to God give us a better understanding of and deeper insights into who God is for us.

Our appreciation of the world around us, of the people who have helped to make us who we are today, and of our experiences can help us realize God in our life. But we must acknowledge the limits of our languages and admit that God is more truly *unlike* than *like*

anything we could say about God, because
God is mystery.

Prayer

In the beginning was God,
Today is God,
Tomorrow will be God.
Who can make an image of God?
God has no body.
God is the word which comes out of your
    mouth.
That word! It is no more,
It is past, and still it lives!
So is God.

—A Pygmy hymn

O Great Spirit, whose voice I hear in the winds,
and whose breath gives life to all the world,
hear me! I am small and weak,
I need your strength and wisdom.
Let me walk in beauty, and make my eyes
ever behold the red and purple sunset.
Make my hand respect the things you have made
and my ears sharp to hear your voice.
Make me wise so that I may understand
the things you have taught my people.

Let me learn the lessons you have hidden
in every leaf and rock.
I seek strength, not to be greater than my
    brother,
but to fight my greatest enemy—myself.
Make me always ready to come to you
with clean hands and straight eyes.
So when life fades, as the fading sunset,
my spirit may come to you without shame.

—An Indian prayer

Grace

I want to in fact—to borrow from the language of
the saints—live "in grace" as much of the time as
possible. By grace, I mean an inner harmony, essen-
tially spiritual.

> —Anne Morrow Lindbergh

[God] gives grace and glory.

> —Psalm 84:11

Grace was in all her steps,
Heaven in her eye,
In every gesture dignity and love.

> —John Milton

We have all experienced grace in our life,
although we sometimes fail to recognize
it. Grace manifests itself in a variety of ways,
but it is a difficult concept to grasp. We speak
of the graceful movements of a dancer or a
deer, the graceful voice of a singer or a song-
bird, the graceful words of a poet. These
things are described as graceful because they
seem to provide beauty without effort, given

freely. But there is more to grace than this; grace is in our everyday life as well.

In spiritual terms grace is an unmerited gift given by God. Grace is divine influence acting to make people morally strong, to increase their holiness, to overcome their evil tendencies, to practice the virtues, and to be of service to the church and all peoples.

We all have contact with people who are individuals of grace. They can be recognized by their conduct, as Jesus said, "You will be able to tell them by their fruits" (Matthew 7:20). They are those who pray often (or live prayerfully) and strive for the best of God's gifts. They are those who are not prejudiced, who carry no grudges, and who share their talents and time with those in need. They are our neighbors, and by grace we can be their neighbor in return.

Prayer

God, as I look over my past, I become more aware of the special graces you have given me. I ask pardon for the graces I have refused, and ask a special grace to receive your gifts in the future. Amen.

Grandparents

A grandfather is a marvelous mixture
   of gentleness and strength.
A grandfather is wisdom with a sense of humor.
A grandfather is kindly, affectionate,
   and an inspiration to his family.
A grandmother is a caring listener with a loving heart.
A grandmother is tenderness, generosity,
   and never-ending patience.
A grandmother enriches her family
   with cherished memories of yesterday.

—Dejean

Every soul that touches yours—
Be it the slightest contact—
Gets there from some good;
Some little grace; one kindly thought;
One aspiration yet unfelt.

—George Eliot

Grandparents can play a special role in the lives of their grandchildren. Those who hope to have a rewarding and lasting relationship with their grandchildren make a special effort to listen, spend time, support, advise, and teach.

With fewer of the day-to-day responsibilities involved in making a living and raising children, grandparents can often afford to be more loving, indulgent, and generous than they had ever been as mother and father. They are often accused of spoiling their grandchildren. It is more likely though that they are celebrating their children's children out of pure love.

Over the past half-century, changes in economics, family values, and family life have caused great changes in the relations between grandparents and grandchildren. In the past, grandparents typically had closer ties with family members. Families tended to be closer geographically. Today people move more frequently from job to job and place to place, taking them away from family members. Divorce, too, makes family members go their separate ways, and so it has had a major effect on grandparents and grandchildren.

No matter how close or how remote grandparents may be geographically, most are specialists in the art of caregiving. They are expert givers and receivers of love and affection, and serve as good influences on their grandchildren. The following are just a few ways grandparents can make a difference in the life of their grandchildren:

- Keep in touch by telephone; children love to get phone calls.
- Maintain a close relationship with the parents of your grandchildren.
- Show an interest in grandchildren's school and social life.
- Attend church with them.
- Send them brief notes; children like to receive mail.
- Plan visits and vacations together, exchange mail throughout the year, and send clippings and photos frequently.

Prayer

For the joys and pleasures I have had in my role as a grandparent, O God, I praise and thank you. I pray for the grace to be a good influence on my grandchildren. I pray also for a change in those grandparents who have been a cause of contention and dissension in family life. Amen.

Happiness

How to gain, how to keep, how to recover happiness
is in fact for most men at all times the secret motive
of all they do and all they are willing to endure.

—William James

The time to be happy is now,
The place to be happy is here,
The way to be happy is to make others so.

—Robert Ingersoll

It is not what you know but who you are that determines happiness.

—Kahlil Gibran

There is more happiness in giving than in receiving.

—Acts of the Apostles 20:35

We were created for happiness. This does
not mean that there will not be periods
of sorrow and pain. Sorrow and pain are
an undeniable part of the human condition.
It would be unwise to put on a happy face
when things go wrong, or to pretend all is well

when we experience poverty and injustice. We certainly do not expect to feel joyful when someone insults or threatens us.

In the face of such realities, how can we pursue happiness?

One sure way toward happiness is to help, support, and care for others in their needs. If we lack an interest in people, we could be in trouble; we could find that happiness eludes us.

If we look back over our life and can honestly say that we have followed the call of God, then we should be happy. John Cardinal Newman gives us this short meditation:

God created me to do Him some definite
    service;
He has committed some work to me
    which He has not committed to another.
I have a mission. I am a link in a chain,
    a bond of connection between
        persons. . . .
Whatever I am cannot be thrown away.
If I am in sickness, my sickness will serve Him;
in perplexity, my perplexity will serve Him.
If I am in sorrow, my sorrow will serve Him.
He does nothing in vain, He knows what He is
    about.

Prayer

God, I ask pardon for the complaining I have done in the past, for the times I have not helped others in need. Give me the special grace to devote my time and energy to the service of others. Amen.

Health

Life is not merely to be alive, but to be well.
                                    —Marcus Martial

Health and intellect are the two blessings of life.
                                    —Menander

A glad heart is excellent medicine,
a depressed spirit wastes the bones away.
                                    —Proverbs 17:22

You will cure me. Restore me to life.
My bitterness turns to well-being.
                                    —Isaiah 38:16–17

If you are a people watcher, you have probably noticed that those in good health display more energy, look better, and tend to have fewer emotional problems. It is no secret that good health depends on many factors, some of which are beyond our control and some of which we can influence or control.

Inherited factors are important elements in our health and well-being. Our air, water, and general environmental conditions also contribute to our health. We have more control, though, over other factors. These include our eating and drinking habits, exercise, the use of drugs, and our social relationships.

The old adage "You are what you eat" still holds true. As we grow older, we tend to have less relish for food, especially if we have to cook only for ourselves or if we don't especially like to eat alone. Those concerned about their eating habits would do well to consult a professionally certified nutritionist. (Do not consult a doctor; doctors generally are not specialists on nutrition.) Many clinics, hospitals, and senior centers have free lectures on nutrition. As for drinking, although a daily drink of alcohol may help digestion and appetite, the habit of drinking because we are lonely, depressed, or sick may be devastating, especially for those taking medications.

There are a lot of reasons to get regular exercise. We live longer, feel better, become more mentally and physically alert, and improve the capacity for enjoyment of life. Exercise programs are available for people of all ages and physical capacities.

I presume that if we could we would like to eliminate all drugs from our system. But, thank God, medications are available for the relief of aches and pains and to maintain the health we have. For the most part, drugs are powerful substances that must be taken as prescribed.

It is always good to be thankful for positive family and other social relationships, and to be grateful for those who visit, call, and help us enjoy holidays and celebrations. Probably nothing is more depressing than loneliness.

Good health brings endurance, relieves tensions, and grants energy and vigor. And that is worth a lot.

Prayer

God, for the good health I have enjoyed in my life, I am grateful. I also thank you for the medicines I need to bear the aches and pains of aging. I pray also for those who care for me and who help me in my times of need. Amen.

Heaven 1

Who, then, can discover what is in the heavens?
—Wisdom 9:16

Heaven means to be one with God.
—Confucius

Heaven is such that all who have lived well, of whatever religion, have a place there.
—Emanuel Swedenborg

Store up treasures for yourselves in heaven.
—Matthew 6:20

The word *heaven,* like the words *God, faith,* and *religion,* has as many meanings as there are people to discuss and argue about it. All the outward-pointing technologies—telescopes, satellites, space shuttles, space probes—have not added much to what we, looking inward, have already speculated.

Discussion about heaven always seems to be associated with the traditional journalistic questions—Who? What? When? Where? Why? How?—Who will go to heaven? What will heaven be like? When will we get there? Where is heaven? Why will a person be there? How will people get there?

Those who will enjoy the delights of heaven are those who have led a good life. Those of evil ways will not be seen among the blessed. Heaven's nature is peaceful, quiet, and happy, without conflicts, setbacks, or disappointments. Those who go to heaven will get there when their souls have been purified. Heaven is not a physical place—God is not limited by physicality—rather, to be in heaven is to experience God's presence fully. Those who are admitted to heaven are admitted because they have accepted the gifts of grace offered by God and have lived a life of service to God and humanity. Finally, heaven is reached by traveling down the path of death.

O happy harbour of the Saints,
O sweet and pleasant soil!
In thee no sorrow may be found,
No grief, no care, no toil.

Ah, my sweet home, Jerusalem,
Would God I were in thee!
Would God my woes were at an end,
Thy joys that I might see!

Quite through the streets, with silver sound,
The flood of Life doth flow;
Upon whose banks on every side
The word of Life doth grow.

(Anonymous)

Prayer

O God, I pray in the words of John Cardinal
Newman:

Support us all the day long of this troublous
life, until the shadows lengthen, and the evening
comes, and the busy world is hushed, and the
fever of life is over, and our work is done. Then
of Thy mercy grant us a safe lodging, and a
holy rest, and peace at the last. Amen.

Heaven 2

It is as Scripture says: What no eye has seen and no ear has heard, what the mind of man cannot visualise; all that God has prepared for those who love him.

—1 Corinthians 2:9

I know a man who . . . was caught up . . . into Paradise and heard words said that . . . cannot and may not be spoken by any human being.

—2 Corinthians 12:2–4

Begin to be now what you will be hereafter.

—Saint Jerome

We are often faced with questions that do not have easy answers—why catastrophes happen; why wars, famine, diseases, family problems, and so on, plague us. I believe that in heaven we will know all the answers. There will be no more mysteries, no secrets. We will finally know how and when the world and all it contains were created.

In my long life, I have had a good deal of time to speculate on the nature of the heavenly afterlife. I believe that in heaven, all will be equally intelligent. The silent oxen will converse with Einstein. All will have the gift of tongues. Or maybe speech will not be necessary, for all will have the gift of mental telepathy. But on the other hand, speech will be essential to the happiness of those who just love to talk, those with the gift of gab.

In heaven we will experience no anxieties, fears, frowns, envy, jealousy, or failure. Everyone will be a success story.

Life on Earth can be very complex, confusing, and busy. But life in heaven will be very simple. All our activities will be reduced to the one for which we were created—to love God and others. Some might say that such an activity could be monotonous and boring for all eternity. But just recall one instance when you performed a perfect act of love, and the happiness that came to you. Such will be eternity—in love forever.

In heaven there will be no banging, rattling, clanging, creaking. Nerves will get a rest while pleasant sounds hold sway. Peace will be enhanced by the smell of air as fresh as spring, further embellished by all the flowers of the earth and by those heavenly blossoms not yet known.

My speculation about heaven leads to this most important point: The long-awaited atmosphere of truth will prevail in heaven. No more lies, fraud, bribes, deceptions. All will be treated with honesty, regardless of their ranking in this earthly life—rich or poor, ignorant or brilliant, saint or sinner—all will be treated the same.

Prayer

I pray in the words of the poet John Donne:

Bring us, O Lord God, at the last awakening into the house and gate of heaven, to enter into that gate and dwell in that house, where there shall be no darkness nor dazzling, but one equal light; no noise nor silence, but one equal music; no fears nor hopes, but an equal possession; no ends nor beginnings, but one equal eternity, in the habitations of Thy majesty and Thy glory, world without end. Amen.

Holy Spirit

It is not you who will be speaking; it is the Holy Spirit.
—Mark 13:11

When the Spirit of truth comes
he will lead you to the complete truth.
—John 16:13

This is the proof that we remain in him and he in us,
that he has given us a share in his Spirit.
—1 John 4:13

"The kingdom of God is within you." By the kingdom of God is meant the grace of the Holy Spirit.
—Saint Seraphim of Sarov

The power of nature sometimes leaves us in awe—earthquakes, volcanoes, floods, tornadoes. We marvel at the human powers that at times are exercised constructively and at other times destructively. Of all the forces at work in the universe, though, no force is as powerful as the Holy Spirit, which moves all humanity and everything in creation.

At the creation of the world, God had a plan. All created things had a purpose in accomplishing God's work. God's spirit is a guiding influence for good.

If the Spirit wants only good, how do we account for the evil in the world? We should remember that we are endowed with free will, a precious gift that allows us the power to choose. We are not slaves or robots. In reality it is just a small minority of people who make bad choices. The majority choose to do the right things. Even the evils of the world are part of the Creator's master plan, though we may not totally understand how evil can work toward the good of all.

The influence of the Spirit is in evidence throughout history. The power of literature, music, art, and drama cannot be measured, but their influence is undeniable. Scientists, with the help of the Spirit, have given us inventions that have changed the world, our lifestyles, and, we hope, enabled us to better serve God and our neighbor.

There are more than five billion people in the world. One outstanding wonder is that I, as an individual, am personally guided by the spirit of God.

Prayer

Holy Spirit, fulfill in me the work begun by the Creator. May the prayer I make on behalf of all the people of the world result in shaping the plan God has for each of us. Amen.

Holy Spirit: Helps, Gifts, and Fruits

The particular manifestation of the Spirit granted to each one is to be used for the general good.
—1 Corinthians 12:7

The Holy Spirit will teach you what you should say.
—Luke 12:12

It is the spirit that gives life.
—John 6:63

I will send my Spirit upon him.
—Matthew 12:18

Every person, created in the image of God, has been endowed with certain qualities, talents, and spiritual gifts. In order to accomplish his or her role on earth and reach his or her final destiny, each individual is influenced by the Spirit that permeates the world.

The helps of the Holy Spirit include the theological virtues, the moral virtues, the gifts of the Holy Spirit, and the fruits of the Spirit.

The theological virtues are faith, hope, and charity. Faith is the virtue by which people believe the truths that God has made known to them. Hope is a virtue by which people trust that God will give them the help they need to reach their goals. Charity is the virtue that allows people to love God and neighbor.

The moral virtues are prudence, justice, fortitude, and temperance. They are called moral virtues because they help persons lead good lives. Prudence helps us to make the right choices, to determine what we must do or not do. Justice prompts us to decide to treat each person with fairness. Fortitude inspires us to do good things even though they may be difficult. Temperance helps us control our desires and inclinations.

The gifts of the Spirit are wisdom, understanding, counsel, fortitude, knowledge, piety, and fear of God. Wisdom is the virtue by which we learn through the teachings of the Scriptures, of Tradition, of the church, and from our mistakes. Understanding is the gift through which we see things as God sees them and use them as God intends. Counsel guides us to make right judgments in our dealings with others. Fortitude gives us the courage to be unafraid to accept challenges and to improve our life. Knowledge enables us to have respect for the truth and to search for values that lead to holiness. Piety is reverence for the things that give glory to God and respect for our neighbor. The fear of God provides wonder and awe for the works that God manifests in the universe.

The fruits of the Holy Spirit appear to be embellishments of the virtues mentioned above. They are attributes that improve our spirituality. According to Tradition these fruits are love, joy, peace, patience, kindness, goodness, gentleness, generosity, faithfulness, modesty, self-control, and chastity.

In our life we have probably had the opportunity to practice all or some of these virtues or fruits. They were present when we had to make important decisions. They were present when we gave glory and praise to God. We experienced them when we had to do some service for others. We felt them when we were on retreat or when we spent time in prayer.

Some of the virtues are more attractive to us than others. The ones that are most appealing are the ones we have developed and that have given us our present degree of spirituality.

Prayer

By the power of the Holy Spirit, may we practice those virtues that give praise to God, service to our neighbor, and a lifestyle of holiness. Amen.

Hope

We always hope; and in all things it is better to hope than to despair. When we return to real trust in God, there will no longer be room in our soul for fear.

—Goethe

I know what plans I have in mind for you. . . . Plans for peace, not for disaster, to give you a future and a hope.

—Jeremiah 29:11

The most universal thing is hope, for hope
stays with those who have nothing else.

—Thales

"Hope" is the thing with feathers—
That perches in the soul—
And sings the tune without the words—
And never stops—at all—

—Emily Dickinson

Many virtues have been exalted by theologians and writers as the most important, the most beautiful, the most necessary, the foundation of all the rest, the first and the last, and so on. Of all the virtues, hope is certainly one of the closest to the center.

In describing hope, two qualities come quickly to mind: hope is powerful, and it is universal. It is a virtue that is deeply implanted in the soul of all peoples. Hope has the power to overcome sickness, poverty, physical disability, criticism, mental difficulties, and even death.

History is filled with people who were filled with hope, who trusted that their desires would be reached. Alexander Graham Bell was laughed at because he claimed he could talk through a wire. We all know what he accomplished. Fyodor Dostoyevski survived four years in a Siberian prison camp and suffered from epilepsy, but still became one of the world's greatest novelists. Beethoven composed great music despite his loss of hearing. Abraham Lincoln failed in business and lost nine elections to public office before becoming president of the United States. Helen Keller, blind and deaf before the age of two, graduated with honors from Radcliffe College and became a renowned author and lecturer.

Through hope we have the confident expectation that if we persevere and trust in God, we will get through life's darkest times.

Fr. James Keller, the founder of the Christophers, has left us these reflections on the virtue of hope:

Hope looks for the good in people instead
  of harping on the worst.
Hope opens doors where despair closes them.
Hope discovers what can be done
instead of grumbling about what cannot.
Hope draws the power from a deep trust in
  God
and the basic goodness of human nature.
Hope "lights a candle" instead of
  "cursing the darkness."

Prayer

God of providence, into your hands I commend my spirit. To you I entrust my temporal and eternal hopes, fears, and desires. I put my trust in you and so shall not be confounded. Amen.

Humility

Anyone who raises himself up will be humbled, and anyone who humbles himself will be raised up.

—Matthew 23:12

The greater you are, the more humbly you should behave.

—Sirach 3:18

He that is humble ever shall
Have God to be his guide.

—John Bunyan

No person will learn anything at all unless he first learn humility.

—Owen Meredith

From the stories of the desert fathers, the early Christian hermits, comes the incident of a young man who asked an elder, "What is humility?" The old man replied, "To do good to those who hurt you." The young man said, "What if I cannot go that far, what should I do?" The elder said, "Go away from them and keep your mouth shut."

Humility is to know oneself, to know one's strengths and weaknesses. A person demonstrates humility by relating honestly with God, oneself, and others.

The opposite of humility is pride or self-deceit. Pride has been the chief cause of misery in every nation and every family since the world began. A person who is proud cannot know God. A proud person always seems to be looking down on others and the world. A person who does that cannot see things that are above.

Humility has never been a very popular virtue, especially in modern society where we tend to pursue our ambitions and rely on our talents, seeking success sometimes at the expense of others. But even in our modern world, humility is the foundation of our spiritual life.

All the holy men and women of the ages have practiced humility. They gave credit and praise, and received the same when it was due.

There is a false humility in which it is considered wrong to accept praise and credit for good work well done. It is false humility to deny we have talents and can do some things better than others can. But a humble person is not disturbed by praise, and does not let it go to his or her head. He or she knows the source of all that is good, and that all praise is in fact intended for that source.

The humble person is not afraid of failure. In fact a humble person is not afraid of anything, because perfect humility implies perfect confidence in the power of God. Humility is the surest sign of strength.

Prayer

"On Humility"

I asked for health, that I might do greater
    things,
I was given infirmity, that I might do better
    things.
I asked for riches, that I might be happy,
I was given poverty, that I might be wise.
I asked for power, that I might have the praise
    of men,
I was given weakness, that I might feel the need
    of God.
I asked for all things, that I might enjoy life,
I was given life, that I might enjoy all things.
I got nothing that I asked for, but everything I
    hoped for.

Almost despite myself, my unspoken prayers
were answered.
I am, among all men, most richly blessed.
—John Cardinal Newman

Humor

The laughter of man is the contentment of God.
—John Weiss

The most wasted day of all is that on which we have not laughed.
—Sébastien R. N. Chamfort

He who is enthroned in the heavens laughs.
—Psalm 2:4

Laughter is part of being whole and thus a part of being holy.
—Muriel James

Humor is a prelude to faith and
Laughter is the beginning of prayer.
—Reinhold Niebuhr

Is there a person in your life who has a great sense of humor? What a joy she or he is to be around. A humorous person creates an atmosphere that touches everyone nearby. A keen sense of humor helps us overlook the unpleasant, tolerate what may be crude, master the unexpected, and outlive the unbearable.

It is said that there are basically seven categories of jokes, the lowest form being the pun. It does not make much difference what kind of humor pleases you; as long as you engage in humor, you will help maintain a sharp and nimble mind. Humor can also prevent, or at least stem the tide of, depression. Recent studies show that it can be a healer of sickness. Experience and common sense tell us that humor produces positive physical and psychological effects. Like exercise, laughter reduces tensions. Many of our ailments can be effectively treated by a "humor prescription." We don't stop laughing because we are old, but we grow old when we lose our sense of humor.

I know I am not alone in believing that Jesus had a great sense of humor. I recall seeing a portrait of Christ by the seashore, laughing. Perhaps he is recalling the time that Peter dared to walk on water and received a dunking for his efforts. Maybe he is remembering his confrontations with the legalistic Pharisees and their ironic rationalizations. He might be recalling the embarrassment of his followers when he rebuked them for not allowing others, such as the little children and the blind man, to approach him. With the challenges Jesus faced, he could hardly have done without a sense of humor!

A good laugh is a sign of love. It is a glimpse of the love that God has for each of us. When the last burst of human laughter resounds before the end, is it too much to imagine that it will resemble the laughter of God?

Prayer

God, a good laugh is joy and sunshine in any language. Grant me a sense of humor to be able to laugh at myself and with others. Amen.

Life

I expect to pass through this world but once. And the good therefore that I can do, or any kindness that I can show to any fellow creature, let me do it now.
—Anonymous

To be what we are, and to become what we are capable of becoming, is the only end of life.
—Robert Louis Stevenson

It is no happiness to live long, no unhappiness to die soon; happy is he who has lived long enough to die well.
—Francis Quarles

Life is neither a good nor an evil; it is simply the place where good and evil exist.
—Seneca

Life is a mystery, whether we are considering the physical, intellectual, psychological, or spiritual aspects of our life.

The human body is a marvelous conglomeration of many complex parts. They function together in ways that are as amazing and mind-boggling as they are taken for granted. Our five senses help us to maintain good health and enjoy the wonders of the universe. They also assist in the learning process and prompt us to avoid things that might be detrimental to our well-being.

The life of our mind is advanced through our intellect, will, memory, and imagination. Think of all the many discoveries that God has allowed us to enjoy due to scientific research and study. Many of the drugs we now need came as a result of many hours of trial and error, one of the many works of the intellect.

As psychological beings we have desires, passions, needs, wants. These can be good or bad, depending on what use we make of them. Experience shows that a balanced psychological life has at least some of the following elements:

- loving and being loved
- respect for oneself and others
- a goal and purpose for living
- helping others
- freedom
- food, shelter, and clothing

We are composed of body and soul, so a spiritual life is needed for a well-balanced human being. The kind of spirituality one has is a matter of choice. Just as it is essential, to varying degrees, to talk to others, so it is necessary to communicate with our God. As food is needed for the body, so prayer is essential for the life of the soul. As the thinking process is needed for intellectual life, so meditation is necessary for spiritual life. And as love, respect, and freedom are essential for a good psychological life, these same elements are needed in our relations with God.

Prayer

God, although I sense that my physical life has declined in my latest years, I thank you for all the aspects of my living and the wonders and beauties I have experienced and enjoyed during my life. Amen. Alleluia.

Living Will

The hour of departure has arrived, and we go our ways—I to die, and you to live. Which is better God only knows.

—Plato

I strove with none, for none was worth my strife;
Nature I loved; and next to Nature, Art.
I warmed both hands before the fire of life;
It sinks, and I am ready to depart.

—Walter Savage Landor

Each of us earns his death, his own death, which belongs to no one else.

—George Seferis

These days there is a good deal of talk about euthanasia, assisted suicide, and the confusion about when death has actually occurred. It seems appropriate that each and every one of us should have something to say about the way we would like to die. However, we can do little about making our wishes known if we put off communicating them before reaching a final state of unconsciousness. The way to determine what care we will receive in our final hours is to complete a document called a living will. The forms for a living will need to be completed while a person is of sound mind, and can be obtained from state boards on aging or family social-service agencies.

Although the directives vary from state to state, the purpose is the same. The living will is a legal document in which a person specifies the types and extent of medical treatment he or she may desire when terminally ill. He or she can also authorize a specific person to make further care decisions for him or her. The living will goes into effect when the individual is unable to make or communicate health-care decisions and when a terminal condition exists.

The living will is an act of charity in the sense that it prevents the burden of deciding how a person should die from being imposed on relatives and physicians. In this way it can provide peace at the end for the one who is dying as well as for the loved ones who must soon grieve.

A living will usually contains specific directives that detail the way the dying person desires to approach his or her death. The following are some examples:

- "At the time it is certain, in the unanimous judgment of three medical specialists, that I have a critical illness that is undoubtedly terminal, I request that I be told of my condition, and that I be asked if I wish the cessation of artificial and extraordinary medical or mechanical means that might prolong my life beyond normal expectations."

- "I ask that pain-relieving drugs be mercifully administered to me in my last illness, even if they may seem to hasten my death. I do not fear death as much as I fear the indignity of deterioration, dependency, and hopeless pain."

- "If I am in this critical and terminal illness stage and unconscious, and it is certain that consciousness will not return, I hereby request that no artificial or mechanical measures be used to prolong my life beyond normal expectations."

The requests contained in a living will must be made while in good health and good spirits. Despite our common resistance to thoughts about dying, it is wise to consider making a living will now, for there may not be a chance later.

Prayer

"Time to Go"

Pardon me, Doctor, but may I die?
I know your oath requires you to try to keep
    me alive
So long as my body is warm and there is a
    breath of life.
But listen, Doc, I've buried my spouse,
My children are grown and on their own.
My friends are all gone, and I want to go, too.
No mortal one should keep me here
When the call from God is unmistakably clear.
I deserve the right to slip quietly away.
My work is done and I am tired.
Your motives are noble, but now I pray
You can read in my eyes what my lips can't say.
Listen to my heart and you'll hear it cry,
Pardon me, Doc, but may I die?

—Anonymous

Loneliness

You will be sad if you are alone.

—Ovid

Solitude vivifies; isolation kills.

—Joseph Roux

What is the worst of woes that wait on age?
What stamps the wrinkle deeper on the brow?
To view each loved one blotted from life's page,
And be alone on earth, as I am now.

—Lord Byron

Loneliness is a common human condition. Everyone feels lonely at one time or another, whether rich or poor, young or old, healthy or sick.

Even if we are involved with others or busy with various projects, we can still become lonely. Lonely feelings are strongest during times of stress and times of change in relations with family and friends. It is important not to become frantic or overly depressed during lonely times. If loneliness is accepted as being natural, it will pass and be replaced by another feeling.

Loneliness and being alone are not necessarily related. Persons may live alone and be alone much of the time without becoming deeply lonely. Such people have a strong sense of self-worth, they live a full, useful life, and they have rich relationships with others. On the other hand, there are those who are not alone but who experience deep feelings of loneliness. They may not realize they are lonely. Because they dread lonely feelings, they attempt to cover them up by becoming depressed, complaining a lot, sleeping constantly, or using drugs. It is wise to be aware of the symptoms of loneliness and to seek ways to overcome it when it seems to be taking over.

Prayer

For the lonely people of the world, I pray. I wish to remember in a special manner those whose family and friends have died. God, grant me the special grace when I become lonely to remember that you are always present. Amen.

Memories

Do not forget the things which you yourselves have seen, or let them slip from your heart as long as you live.

—Deuteronomy 4:9

Memory: what wonders it performs in preserving and storing up things gone by.

—Plutarch

Everybody needs his memories. They keep the wolf of insignificance from the door.

—Saul Bellow

The dictionary gives a very simple definition of *reminisce:* to recall or remember. We have a gift called memory that allows us to reminisce.

Reminiscence is a natural process of recalling past events. People in all cultures and all walks of life can and do reminisce. We can reminisce privately, or we can share our memories with others who have had similar experiences or who might stand to learn something from our experience. When a person reminisces, she or he is usually influenced by emotions such as anger, sadness, or happiness. A particular emotion in the present can evoke certain memories, and memories can evoke particular emotions in the present.

Our memories can give us meaning, especially at a period in life when our present activities are limited by age and physical capacity. Take a few moments to do some private reminiscing. Consider sharing some of the following memories with others:

- What are your memories of your place of birth?
- What do you remember of your parents and your grandparents?
- Recall some important experiences shared with your siblings.
- Recall other relatives and friends.
- What place did religion have in your family?
- In what sort of town or city did you grow up?
- What schools did you attend?

- Recall your first job. How much did you earn, and what did you do with your first paycheck?
- What did you do for entertainment?
- What historical events do you remember?
- How did you spend holidays such as Thanksgiving, Christmas, New Year's, Easter, and the Fourth of July?

Prayer

God, whatever happened to the good old days? Everything seems so different now. However, I thank you for my memory, through which I am able to live twice by recalling the persons, places, and things that give meaning to my life today. Amen.

Miracles

Miracles are for those who believe in them.
—W. G. Benham

I have seen no more evident monstrosity and miracle in the world than myself.
—Michel de Montaigne

The heavens declare the glory of God,
the vault of heaven proclaims his handiwork.
—Psalm 19:1

An act of God was defined as "something which no reasonable man could have expected."
—Sir Alan Herbert

I agree with Montaigne, quoted above, that I am a miracle. (I'll reserve judgment on the monstrosity part.) When I consider all the parts of the human body and how they function, I wonder at the fact that they did not wear out a long time ago.

Physical miracles occur every day. One example would be the process of healing.

Where would we be if all the injuries and illnesses of our lifetime did not heal? Think of the morning when you wake up, finally feeling better after a period of illness—that day most certainly feels like a miracle!

In nature we experience the miracle of planting, cultivating, and harvesting. We see the miracle of new growth where a forest has burned to the ground. Throughout the various seasons of the year, we witness miracles of death and rebirth that are affected by the orbit of the earth around the sun.

When we reflect on the wonders of the twentieth century in medicine, science, space, and so on, we have to admit that miracles are taking place in our very presence. And don't forget the social miracles—it has been said, for example, that one of the greatest miracles of this century is the Alcoholics Anonymous program, which is responsible for saving countless lives.

Try to see the miracles in life.

Prayer

God of all, help me to see the miracles in my life, to never take for granted the sunrise, the trees that bud anew each spring, the stars in their glory on a summer night, the golden trees of autumn. Help me to see the miracles in the people around me and to be a miracle in my relations with others. Amen.

Music

The truest expression of a people is in its dance and its music. Bodies never lie.

—Agnes de Mille

Music is well said to be the speech of angels.

—Thomas Carlyle

The language of tones belongs equally to all mankind, and melody is the absolute language in which the musician speaks to every heart.

—Richard Wagner

What would the world be without music? For the most part, it would be dull, drab, and desperate. God created us with the gift to appreciate music, and a chosen few have the gift to create music for the rest of us.

The type of music one enjoys depends upon one's personality, education, and mood at a particular time. There is so much to choose from: classical, popular, country, jazz, folk, and rock are some basic categories, and the diversity within each category is remarkable.

When it comes to different types of music, one person's pleasure may be another's poison, but that is part of the wonder of music. If music is, as Thomas Carlyle said, the speech of angels, then angels speak in many languages.

If you are one of the fortunate ones who plays or has played an instrument, then consider yourself one of God's chosen ones. You probably annoyed yourself and others as a beginner, but as time went on, you enjoyed playing for yourself, with others, and for others. The gift of music is at its best when it is shared.

If people have always associated music with God, it is probably because they saw it as a way of communication between the mundane and the divine. Music creates a new space wherever it is heard, and often creates an atmosphere for prayer—from the prayer of quiet to the prayer of ecstatic dancing.

We need music because in many ways it brings out the best in humanity. Music is within the listener. Different kinds of music evoke different emotions in different people in the various stages of their life. Listen for the music of life.

Prayer

For the musicians, past and present, and their works of music, I am grateful, God. May the melodies they have given us be a source of love, joy, hope, humor, and peace. Amen.

Nature

I love to think of nature as an unlimited broadcasting station, through which God speaks to us every hour, if we will only tune in.

—George Washington Carver

This grand show is eternal. It is always sunrise somewhere; the dew is never all dried at once; a shower is forever falling; vapor is ever rising. Eternal sunrise, eternal sunset, eternal dawn and gloaming, on seas, on continents and islands, each in its turn, as the round earth rolls.

—John Muir

If you get simple beauty and nought else,
you get about the best God invents.

—Robert Browning

There is no creature, regardless of its apparent insignificance, that fails to show us something of God's goodness.

—Thomas à Kempis

Recall the times you have visited a zoo, a botanical garden, or a museum of natural history. You will remember the mammals, great and small; the birds of exotic colors; and the other animals of various sizes and shapes. Perhaps a certain species comes to mind whose habits, habitat, and means of survival attracted your attention. On the other hand, you may have been drawn to replicas of animals that have become extinct.

Any encounter with nature can be a source of prayer or meditation. It is a matter of using our senses, imagination, and memory to assist in contemplating the work of God in nature. We can plainly see the care God has for creation in the beauty exhibited in the realm of the flowers, plants, and trees. We see God's care in the ways the intricate net of creation provides for the survival of such a rich diversity of creatures. We should oppose the ways in which people have acted contrary to the laws of nature for profit, and recall the saying of Francis Bacon, "Nature is not governed except by obeying her."

The sun, moon, planets, stars, rain, snow, floods, earthquakes, volcanoes are all part of

God's plan. We may not fully understand God's reasons for some of the pieces of creation, but we should never forget whose they are.

Prayer

O God, I thank you for this earth, our home, for the wide sky and the blessed sun, for the salt seas and the running waters, for the everlasting hills and the never-resting winds, for the trees and the grass underfoot. Amen.

Peace

To the utmost of your ability, be at peace with everyone.

—Romans 12:18

The peace sown by peacemakers brings a harvest of justice.

—James 3:18

Five great enemies to peace inhabit within us: viz., avarice, ambition, envy, anger, and pride. If those enemies were to be banished, we should infallibly enjoy perpetual peace.

—Petrarch

Peace is not an absence of war, it is a virtue, a state of mind, a disposition for benevolence, confidence, justice.

—Benedict de Spinoza

A study of the history of war shows that Petrarch, quoted above, is right. Any confrontation that occurs is usually caused by some combination of these vices: avarice, ambition, envy, anger, and pride.

Many people are of the opinion that if all the weapons' factories in the world were closed, there would be no more wars. This is far from the truth. Spiritual leaders and other authoritative figures have often maintained that weapons, whether they are nuclear missiles or fists, do not of themselves cause wars. Wars are waged by the people who use the weapons, no matter how primitive or modern those weapons may be.

In the Bible, peace is a very broad concept. It goes well beyond the notion of peace as the absence of war. Peace refers to a state of being intact, of being complete. It fosters a tranquil life. It is harmony with others, ourselves, and God. It means blessing, rest, glory, unity, concord, and quiet.

Peace and happiness go together in the Scriptures. To be in good health and to be at peace are two parallel expressions. Peace means contentment and joy.

Prayer

God, may we trust in the power of good to overcome evil and the power of love to overcome hatred. Help us to devote our lives to the task of peace in order to fulfill the end for which we were created. Amen.

Person

His gaze scrutinises the children of Adam.
—Psalm 11:4

Every moment of my life is in your hands.
—Psalm 31:15

God has created me to do him some definite service.
He has assigned some work to me which he has not
assigned to another. . . . He has not created me for
nothing.
—Alaska Radio Mission

The spirit in every being is made manifest
in the eyes, and in the bodily movements
and gestures. Our appearance, our words,
our actions are never greater than ourselves.
—Kahlil Gibran

It is estimated that over five billion human
beings live on the face of the earth. Yet God
cares for each one individually. I am as important to God as any other person.

We each have been endowed with special
gifts and talents for our own welfare and to

serve others. These others have endowments to be used for the same purposes. This is one of the marvels of creation—no two people on earth are exactly the same, not even identical twins.

At times I have wished to be someone else or to have lived in some other century or to have resided in some other country. But here I am as God made me and where God wants me to be. If I refuse to accept myself as God made me, I will never have a full life.

I must also accept the limitations that come with the aging process. These limitations are not obstacles to my succcess; they are signs from God of the path I should take for the rest of my life.

Prayer

God, of all gifts to humanity, I wish to thank you for all the good you have done through me, some of which I now recall. I offer these things in your name. Amen.

Poets, Poetry, and Prayer

A poet is a painter of the soul.
                                    —Isaac D'Israeli

God's most candid critics are those of His children whom He has made poets.
                                    —Sir Walter Raleigh

Poetry is the language of the gods.
                                    —Samuel Rogers

Poetry is faith. . . . The test of the poet is the power to take the passing day and hold it up to a divine reason. . . . Poetry is the consolation of mortal man.
                                    —Ralph Waldo Emerson

We all have had some exposure to poetry. Some people make poetry a part of daily life; others avoid it altogether. It is likely that our attitude toward poetry was shaped early by a teacher or a parent who made us see poetry as either vital or as drudgery.

But whatever attitude we take, we must admit that poets present us with special messages that speak to us of love, beauty, sorrow, justice, morality, nature, life, death, and God. The essence of poetry is to reveal the truth and to lead the reader to the truth.

Poetry affects our thinking, which leads to inspiration. And inspiration is the thinking of the heart. Inspiration involves the emotions, which in turn involve the whole person—mind and body.

The authentic poet has a message to give to others. The authentic poet is not for herself or himself but for others. She or he is a sort of prophet sent to enlighten others about the will of God, truth, love, beauty, and the affirmation of life in general.

Prayer

God, help me to better appreciate the poetic sayings I encounter in my life. In the future, grant me grace to read more poetry as a part of my prayer life. Amen.

Prayer: Balance

Prayer crowns God with honor and glory due His name.

—Thomas Benton Brooks

Our prayers should be for blessings in general, for God knows best what is best for us.

—Roy L. Smith

Four things which are not in Thy treasury,
I lay before Thee, Lord, with this petition:
My nothingness, my wants,
My sins, and my contrition.

—Robert Southey

Give thanks to [God], for he is good,
his faithful love lasts for ever.

—Psalm 107:1

The church teaches that all prayers fall into one of four categories: praise, thanksgiving, petition, and contrition.

In prayer, sometimes we give praise to God simply because God deserves it. At other times, we give God thanks for favors or goodness received. In petition, we ask God for some favor, because we are always in need of help. And we are sinners, so through contrition we ask for forgiveness for the sins we have committed.

A few years back, a survey asked participants which category of prayer they used most during a given month. Results showed that petition was employed ten times more than contrition. Praise and thanksgiving fell in between, with more attention given to thanksgiving than to praise. It seems that our prayer life may be somewhat unbalanced if we concentrate on only one or two types of prayer. It should be our aim to include all types of prayer in our daily practice of communicating with God.

The Scriptures tell us little about how to pray. They simply tell us to speak to God as we would to anyone with whom we are well acquainted. Prayer need not become an exercise in memorization. Let's talk plainly to God about our lives, relationships, hopes, joys, and disappointments.

Prayer

God, I praise you for all the wonders you have given to me. I thank you for having given me life and preserved it for these many years. I ask for your continued blessings on myself and those I love, and I ask your forgiveness for the sins I have committed. Amen.

Prayer: Listening

Never want for a better time or place to pray. God hears you wherever you are.

—Anonymous

Let your prayer be completely simple, for the publican, the prodigal son, and the thief were reconciled to God by a single phrase.

—Saint John Climacus

Prayer does not change God, but changes him who prays.

—Søren Kierkegaard

In your prayers do not babble as the gentiles do, for they think that by using many words they will make themselves heard.

—Matthew 6:7

So many articles, poems, dissertations, and books are written on prayer that they could fill a library of their own. At the heart of the topic of prayer, however, is the simple truth that prayer is intended to bring about a closer relationship with God. It is always good to recall, renew, and revive some of the types, characteristics, and qualities of prayer that can make this goal a reality.

We often think of prayer as verbal activity—we talk to God. Such prayer is good and fruitful. But we ought not to forget about the importance of listening during our prayer time. Throughout our life we have put so much emphasis on saying something during prayers that we have neglected listening prayer.

God speaks to us all the time, but we are inclined not to listen. It may be that God speaks in a language we do not want to hear. It may be that God's language does not jibe with our wants and desires, and so we resist it.

How do I know when God speaks to me? One way is by reading the Scriptures, for God speaks to us through them, telling us the right way to live with others and all creation.

God speaks to us as well through the people, events, and experiences of our life. The people in my life have helped me better relate to God. The positive and negative happenings of the past are occasions that have brought me closer to God. In the created world, I see another revelation of God's presence. And we can best understand what God is saying to us through people, events, and creation by taking time in our prayer life to be quiet and listen to what God is trying to say.

Prayer

God, teach me what it means to listen to you in my prayer time, through the Scriptures, people, events, and creation, so that in all circumstances I may be closer to you. Amen.

Presence of God

Here God lives among human beings. He will make his home among them.
>   —Revelation 21:3

God enters by a private door into every individual.
>   —Ralph Waldo Emerson

I would rather walk with God in the dark than go alone in the light.
>   —Mary Gardiner Brainard

I am with you always; yes, to the end of time.
>   —Matthew 28:20

In Proverbs 15:3 we read, "The eyes of Yahweh are everywhere." Many of us were taught in our early years that God sees all our actions. This probably brought on guilt feelings when we were up to no good. But the expression does not mean that God is spying on us. By being omnipresent, God is here to help us, to change us, whether we are at our worst or our best.

It is not necessary that we feel God's presence. We must believe God is here. When we are in the presence of others, we communicate with them either by words or actions. Why do we find it difficult to talk to God, who is always present? Why do we think of God as being present only when we are in church or at prayer? God must be present to us at all times to sustain the physical, psychological, and spiritual aspects of our life.

God rejoices to be considered our friend, to be known as one who loves us just as we are. God is with us wherever we are: on a walk, at parties, on vacation, in the car, out shopping. God is in any activity in which we are involved. Recognize God wherever you go.

Prayer

God, today I ask for a very special favor: for a firm belief and a conscious awareness that you are always in my presence to assist me in my journey of life. Amen.

Revelation

As your word unfolds, it gives light,
and even the simple understand.
                                    —Psalm 119:130

You will teach me the path of life.
                                    —Psalm 16:11

If God has spoken, why is the universe not convinced?
                                    —Percy Bysshe Shelley

The process of Revelation has been going on since the beginning of the world. Adam and Eve, as we read in Genesis, received a Revelation of God, and through the ages God has continued to be revealed to all humanity.

Even after the sin of Adam and Eve, God did not abandon them and their descendants, but made several agreements of hope of salvation and forgiveness through the various stages of history. God used the prophets, leaders, and holy men and women to keep hope alive in the hearts of all people until the final Revelation: Jesus Christ, God's Son.

With the appearance of Christ on Earth, there is no further Revelation as far as God is concerned. However, Revelation will never be complete in its relation to the nations of the earth. It remains for all peoples to grasp the full significance of this Revelation over the course of the centuries.

The common sources of Revelation are the Scriptures and Tradition. Sacred Scripture is the word of God as it is put in writing by the inspiration of the Holy Spirit. Tradition transmits the word of God, which has been entrusted to those appointed by God and their successors, so that they may faithfully preserve, teach, and spread the truth.

If Revelation as such stopped two thousand years ago, what is to be said of the apparitions such as Guadalupe, Lourdes, Fatima, and more recently Medjugorje? These are called "private" revelations. It is not their role to improve or complete the final Revelation, which is Christ; they help us to live more fully the Revelation of God in a certain period of history.

Prayer

It is with a heart full of gratitude that I recall the various ways by which you, O God, have revealed yourself to me and to others. I see you in the Scriptures, in Tradition, in private revelations, in nature, in people, and in the sciences. May I use them for your honor and glory. Amen.

Saints 1

Saints are really sinners who just keep on trying.
—Alaska Radio Mission

Saint, n. a dead sinner revised and edited.
—Ambrose Bierce

There are many canonized on earth, who shall never be saints in heaven.
—Sir Thomas Brown

Throughout history men and women of all races, creeds, and lifestyles have been born with the spirit of truth in them; we classify them as saints.

What makes a person a saint? Because each individual is unique and lives in different circumstances, saintliness is expressed in a variety of ways. That is why there is such a wide range of saints: kings and beggars, scholars and soldiers, the single and the married, popes, artists, alcoholics, religious. They all devote themselves to God and enjoy and appreciate the good things of this world to varying degrees.

"You will be able to tell them by their fruits" (Matthew 7:16). Saints must have certain signs of holiness: they should be prayerful, loving, forgiving, just, faithful to their calling, peaceful, joyful, and compassionate.

Many people choose a patron saint. The choice may be based on one's given name or occupation, the saint's country of origin, or just personal taste. Cities and countries sometimes have patron saints as well. Universal saints, such as Mary and Joseph, receive the devotion of people from many nations and walks of life.

We honor the saints because they have followed the Way, the Truth, and the Life. As we study their lives, we hear them say to us, "Be ye followers of me as I am of Christ."

Prayer

Heavenly saints, I pray today for the special grace I need to become more Christlike. I also pray that my friends and relatives receive the special graces they need to overcome their trials. Amen.

Saints 2

The way of this world is to praise dead saints and persecute living ones.
> —Nathaniel Howe

There is only one sadness: not to be a saint.
> —Georges Bernanos

Every human being is called to holiness. No religion or church has a monopoly on it.
> —*Christopher News Notes*

Many religions recognize the existence of the communion of saints. In this community are saints (canonized or not) who have arrived at their heavenly home, saints who have died but are delayed in purgatory, and potential saints still living on Earth.

Since all persons are called to be holy, we can include in the communion of saints people of every race, culture, and creed who have committed themselves to the task of making a better world by promoting God's justice, mercy, and peace. Take a good look and you will find saints all around you, not only in your own society but in other countries throughout the world.

In the communion of saints, we have a powerful source of assistance and compassion. The saints in heaven help those on earth who are still struggling. They listen to the prayers of the living to relieve the sufferings of those in purgatory. Those in purgatory offer their sufferings for those on Earth, and for their own release. Those on Earth pray for the release of the suffering souls, and offer prayers to saints for an increase in holiness. There is no end to the good that can be accomplished through the compassion of the communion of saints.

Each year the Christian churches commemorate the feast of All Saints on the first of November. All Saints' Day honors all persons who have arrived in heaven, whether they have been canonized or not. On this day we honor those of our own family and our neighbors. It is ecumenical and enriching to honor saints from other traditions as well. The communion of saints transcends physical and national boundaries, to the benefit of us all.

Prayer

God of all, I pray for all peoples of the earth, living and dead. Grant them the special graces they need to become holy and part of your saintly communion. Amen.

The Scriptures 1

Many things in the Bible I cannot understand; many things in the Bible I only think I understand; but there are many things in the Bible I cannot misunderstand.

—Anonymous

The Scriptures teach us the best way of living, the noblest way of suffering, and the most comfortable way of dying.

—John Flavel

The entire Bible has been read, studied, and critiqued more than any other book on the face of the earth. It is also ranked number one among the best-sellers through the years.

Although the Bible is a prime topic for scholars, exegetes, and commentators, whose studies can be of great benefit, the words of the Scriptures were preserved for ordinary persons like you and me. We may have difficulty understanding certain parts of the Bible, such as the historical and prophetic books of the Old Testament and the Book of Revelation in the New Testament. Consulting commentaries can be most helpful when we find ourselves confused. Books of instruction, such as Wisdom and Proverbs, are much more accessible and provide many lessons that can help in daily life. The Book of Psalms is a prayer book that covers every type of prayer and the full range of human emotion. In the New Testament, the Gospels give us fascinating accounts of the life, death, and Resurrection of Jesus Christ. We may marvel at his miracles or be humbled by his teachings, but we will be hard-pressed to remain untouched by him.

Keep in mind that the Scriptures were written by persons inspired by the Holy Spirit to preserve God's message for all ages. We should look upon any part of the Bible that we read as a message, a letter from God. All Scripture is inspired by God and can be profitably used for teaching, for refuting error, for guiding people's lives, and for teaching them to be holy (see 2 Timothy 3:16).

Prayer

Holy spirit of God, as I read the sacred Scriptures, be near me to guide me to understand your word as it applies to my life. Amen.

The Scriptures 2

Nothing will repay one so much as the constant study and meditation of Holy Scripture.
—Paul Claudel

You are wrong, because you understand neither the scriptures nor the power of God.
—Matthew 22:29

Nobody ever outgrows scripture; the book widens and deepens with our years.
—Charles H. Spurgeon

Why should we consider the daily reading of some part of the Bible as a portion of our prayer life?

God speaks to us first. This fundamental truth makes it possible for us to pray to God. Praying with the Scriptures requires a faith that it is God speaking to us. Reading the Bible is like sitting with friends and sharing our scrapbooks. The Scriptures are God's way of sharing divine life with us.

The question often arises, What part of the Bible should I read on a daily basis? This is a matter of choice. One suggestion is to use the liturgical readings of the day, usually consisting of passages from each Testament. These readings encompass most of the Bible in the course of a three-year cycle. The listing of readings can be found in pamphlets from religious bookstores or obtained from a pastor, deacon, or pastoral minister.

The guidelines that follow may help your praying with the Bible:

- Set aside a specific time each day in a quiet place.
- Say a prayer to the Holy Spirit for inspiration.
- Read the chosen passage slowly; read it again if needed.
- Listen to what God is saying to you; apply it to your life in a practical way.
- Thank and praise God for this opportunity to listen to God's voice.
- Pray for your personal needs and those of relatives and friends.

Prayer

For the grace to be able to read the word of God every day, I thank you, Holy Spirit. May you continue to teach me how to relate to God and to all I meet. Amen.

Sin

If we say, "We have no sin," we are deceiving ourselves.

—1 John 1:8

Sin is not hurtful because it is forbidden, but it is forbidden because it is hurtful.

—Benjamin Franklin

Let the one among you who is guiltless be the first to throw a stone at her.

—John 8:7

Throughout history peoples have recognized the existence of good and evil, of right and wrong. One of our God-given gifts is our conscience, which helps us to see for ourselves what is right and what is wrong.

The human conscience develops with help from many sources as an individual matures. This help comes from grandparents, parents, teachers, and other significant people in one's life. Help comes too from the religious and philosophical traditions we encounter. From the vantage point of age, we can recall the many times in our childhood when we received approval or disapproval for our conduct, and this played a part in the growth of conscience.

The greatest obstacle to a happy life lies within ourselves: it is a malformed or poorly functioning conscience. We can probably remember the first time we felt guilt or remorse as a result of some wrongdoing. This feeling was a result of our conscience at work. On the other hand, we might recall positive feelings that followed a good action on our part. A lifetime of such actions, good and bad, defines in many respects who we are and what we mean to the people around us.

Take a few moments to recall some incidents in which your conscience guided you to a greater sense of well-being.

Prayer

Forgive, O God, the sins of my youth and those of my riper years, the sins of my soul and the sins of my body, the sins I know and remember and those I have forgotten. In your mercy forgive them all. Amen.

Spirituality 1

Real holiness has love for its essence, humility for its clothing, the good of others for its employment, and the honor of God as its end.

—Nathaniel Emmons

To be religious is to give your life so that the world may be more beautiful, more just, more at peace; it is to prevent egotistical and self-serving ends from disrupting this harmony of the whole.

—Arturo Paoli

To be holy and not happy is a contradiction.

—Anonymous

The dictionary tells us that the word *spirituality* means to relate to or to affect the spirit; to refer to sacred matters; to be concerned with religious values; to be attached to holy persons, places, or things. With such a range of definitions, it is no surprise that there are many ways of being spiritual. All these ways are important; one or more is likely to become the basis of our own personal growth.

Through the centuries we have witnessed many schools or movements of spirituality. The hermits, the mystics, the Jesuits, the Dominicans, the Franciscans, the indigenous peoples of many lands, and the Eastern religions have given us a variety of insights about the spiritual life. From these sources we have developed our own spirituality, and it is a good sign if we are still searching. In order to become genuine spiritual human beings, we must seek and find meaning in life in general, in death in particular, and in the various events of our daily living.

In our modern, technological age, we may be inclined to try to measure, evaluate, or research our spirituality. In fact it is difficult to measure our spiritual life. Spirituality is an art, not a science. To compare our spirituality today with the way it was when we were young—or even last year—is wasted energy because we are constantly undergoing change. Our spirituality is such that it cannot be separated from the biological, psychological, social, material, and religious aspects of our life. As these change, so does our spirituality. Through all these changes is one constant: we can unite ourselves with God, communicate with God, and aspire to do God's will.

Prayer

I thank you, God, for the gift of spirituality, which brings me the joy and happiness of praising you and of serving those in need. Amen.

Spirituality 2

Holiness appeared to me to be of a sweet, pleasant, charming, serene, calm nature, which brought an inexpressible purity, brightness, peacefulness, and ravishment to the soul.

—Jonathan Edwards

We are well aware that God works with those who love him, . . . and turns everything to their good.

—Romans 8:28

The serene, silent beauty of a holy life is the most powerful in the world, next to the might of the Spirit of God.

—Blaise Pascal

The term *spirituality* is so complex in meaning that it may at times be confusing and misleading. It can be related to our prayer life, our volunteer work, our piety, our fidelity to our devotions, our social life, our personality. It can be all or none of these. One simple way of understanding what is at the heart of spirituality is to see that it is concerned with our ability, through our attitudes and actions, to relate to others, to ourselves, and to God. Let's look briefly at spirituality in terms of these three relationships.

In our relations with others:
- Holiness is not the result of doing good; I do good because of my spirituality.
- Spirituality does not follow because I am kind and patient; I am kind and patient because I am holy.
- I do not acquire spirituality after a lifetime of service; I am a servant of others because I am holy.

In our relations with ourselves:
- Spirituality is not acquired by building character; I build character because of my spirituality.
- The habit of prayer does not necessarily result in my holiness; I pray regularly because I am holy.
- Holiness is not a reward because I avoid evil; I avoid the wrong because I am holy.

In our relations with God:

- Holiness does not occur because I obey the laws of God; I am obedient because I am holy.
- Being a spiritual person does not follow because I praise and glorify God; I praise God because I am holy.

Our real work in this life is to grow spiritually. We do this by always following the path of what is good. When we were younger, we were probably caught up in the culture of materialism, believing that having material possessions somehow defined our worth. As the years passed, we began to realize that the material should be secondary to the spiritual. The material things we need most are those that help us to attain the spiritual.

Prayer

God, grant me the graces I need in my relations with others, myself, and God, so that I may grow in holiness. Amen.

Suffering 1

Have pity on me, Yahweh, see my affliction.
—Psalm 9:13

If you suffer, thank God! It is a sure sign you are alive.
—Elbert Hubbard

All that we suffer in the present time is nothing in comparison with the glory which is destined to be disclosed for us.
—Romans 8:18

There is no mortal whom sorrow and disease do not touch.
—Euripides

Why do I have to suffer so much? Why is this happening to me? What did I do wrong to have to bear this? Why is there so much suffering in the world if God wants us to be happy? If God is all-powerful and can do all things, why does suffering exist at all? These are age-old questions for which humans have long sought satisfactory answers.

To reflect on the meaning of suffering in general is no easy task. In truth, we can only begin to understand our own suffering, much less the suffering of others and the world. How many times does it happen that a visitor to a sick person will say, "I know just how you feel; I went through the same thing myself." The intention to show empathy may be praiseworthy, but the statement is totally false and should never be uttered. The suffering of each person is a personal and unique experience that cannot be duplicated by any other individual. No one else will ever be able to understand your suffering completely, and no one else can relieve you of your suffering. In the same way, no one will be able to bear your burden as you are willing to bear it.

There does not seem to be a general or universal meaning that can be applied to all the different kinds of suffering. One person's suffering cannot be compared with the suffering of another, because suffering is very subjective.

Because suffering is unique, the meaning of one's suffering is also unique. This meaning relates to the circumstances that are behind it. For example, some suffering may be more readily accepted and understood when it takes place as part of the aging process than if it had occurred during an earlier stage of life.

One thing about suffering seems to be clear and understandable: people who have never suffered or who have suffered very little during their younger years will have more trouble finding meaning in suffering as adults or older persons. Friends and family and faith in God are certain to be helpful to those who are coping with suffering and misfortune.

The meaning of suffering is not found in the response to the questions raised at the beginning of this meditation. The meaning is better found in the answers to questions such as these: How can I improve my life with my suffering? What can I do with it? What can I make of the pain that I now endure? How can I profit from the sufferings of others?

Prayer

God, teach me patience while I enjoy good health and when I am sick and suffering. Lighten my burden and strengthen my endurance. Amen.

Suffering 2

Where there is sorrow, there is holy ground.
—Oscar Wilde

In suffering one learns to pray best of all.
—Harold Bosley

Physical ills are the taxes laid upon this wretched life; some are taxed higher, and some lower, but all pay something.
—Lord Chesterfield

Suffering can be experienced in a variety of ways and intensities. Physical suffering may result from chronic or sudden illness, from injury, from the weather, from surgery, or from fatigue, among many other causes. Emotional suffering also has many possible causes: fear, anxiety, the death of a loved one, a move to a new place, dissatisfaction, loneliness, worries, mental-health issues.

A third kind of suffering is spiritual suffering. It is the suffering we experience when we seem to be out of touch with God, when we cannot pray, when we sense our mortality, or when we feel guilt and fear because of past failures.

All these kinds of suffering vary from person to person. They may even vary within a single individual at different times. However, all these types are interrelated and influence one another. Spiritual or emotional suffering is usually associated with each incident of physical suffering we experience.

Take, for example, a man who has lost his hand in an accident. He will experience obvious physical suffering. He is likely also to suffer emotionally because of the anger aroused by his condition or the anxiety caused by being stared at in public. He may also suffer spiritually if he feels anger at God over his loss, thereby distancing himself from God.

Suffering invariably brings on a state of depression, to greater or lesser degrees. To find meaning in any suffering, one must first come out of the depression. In attempting to do so, one must have patience and must depend on God's help to cope with and accept suffering with a positive spirit.

Prayer

God, in your love you healed the sick, made the blind see, the deaf hear, and the lame walk. In your mercy look kindly on us who are sick and suffering. If it is not your will that we be cured, help us to bear our suffering with patience and courage. Amen.

Time 1

O God! Methinks it were a happy life,
To be no better than a homely swain;
To sit upon a hill, as I do now,
To carve out dials, quaintly, point by point,
Thereby to see the minutes how they run,
How many make the hour full complete;
How many hours bring about the day;
How many days will finish up the year;
How many years a mortal man may live.
—William Shakespeare

Most of us have probably wondered from time to time why we were born at the time we were. Why did we come into existence at a particular time and place in history? Why not in a different country and a different century? From all eternity God determined that I was to enjoy the wonders of the twentieth century. If God wanted me to be in any other place at any other time, I would have been there. According to God's plan, I am in the right place at the right time.

In the words of French missionary Stephen Grellet, we "expect to pass through this world but once." I am now experiencing my once-forever passage through life in an age that has been dominated by changes. It has been estimated that the changes that have occurred in this century have outnumbered those that happened in the three previous centuries.

During my sojourn I have witnessed or experienced two major wars and several lesser ones, the Depression, the Holocaust and other genocides, famines, the partitioning of Russia, the space program, great advances in science and medicine, the emphasis on education, the Second Vatican Council, spiritual renewal, the age of protest, and on and on. I have also the experiences of my personal life, my family, and my career. All have made me what I am at this moment in time.

All this has not happened by chance. It was planned before the world came into existence. God saw this as my time, the time when I could best honor God and serve others.

Prayer

God, I have been disturbed at times by the troubles and problems of the world. Some of the changes are not to my liking. Grant me the grace to accept the changes that are part of your plan and to avoid those that are not necessary for salvation. Amen.

Time 2

Time is Eternity begun.

—James Montgomery

Time is the image of eternity.

—Diogenes Laertius

We feel and know we are eternal.

—Benedict de Spinoza

It is baffling to consider God's enormous task: to take care of every person on the face of the earth in every moment—a task involving billions of people. The thing to notice here comes in the words *in every moment*. Human life happens moment by moment. One moment disappears before the next one starts.

But God does not work in time. God does not exist moment by moment. God exists and acts in eternity. All events—past, present, and future in human terms—are "ever present" to God. The events that happened during the year you were born are as present to God as the events of the next century. This is a mystery but also a revelation. With God there is no past and future, there is only eternity. Hence, everything that has ever taken place and that will ever take place is always present to God.

It might be said that now is always and always is now. Time and eternity are inseparable. And the events of our earthly life, our life in time, are the preamble to our eternal life.

Prayer

God, you made me to exist forever. May the time I live on this earth be a worthy preparation for the life reserved for me in eternity. Amen.

Truth

You will come to know the truth,
and the truth will set you free.

—John 8:32

Truth is something that must be known
in the mind, accepted in the heart,
and enacted in life.

—Kahlil Gibran

Truth is the secret of eloquence and of all virtue, the
basis of moral authority; it is the highest summit of
art and life.

—Giovanni Battista Amiel

God has blessed humanity by making each
person truthful by nature. Truth in human action and speech is called truthfulness,
sincerity, or candor. It is a virtue that shows
itself in words and deeds. It is a safeguard
against duplicity and hypocrisy. People could
not live with one another if there was not a
certain amount of confidence that they could
trust one another.

The virtue of truth gives to another his or her just due. Truthfulness keeps a balance of what ought to be expressed and what should be kept secret; it entails honesty and discretion. In the name of justice, a person owes it to another to manifest the truth.

Many people in all ages have declared the truth at the cost of life. Even in our present time, many still suffer persecution and torture while defending the truth of the dignity of the human person.

The most direct offense against the truth is lying. To lie is to speak or act against the truth in order to lead into error someone who has the right to know the truth. By its nature, lying is to be condemned. It is to misuse the gift of speech, whereas the purpose of speech is to communicate the known truth to others.

Charity and respect for the truth should dictate what information should be given or withheld. The good and safety of others, respect for privacy, and the common good are sufficient reasons for being silent about what should not be known.

Prayer

God, for the many times through fear, shame, gain, or spite I have not told the truth, I ask forgiveness. In the future grant me the grace to be sincere in all my dealings with others. Amen.

Virtue

The fruits of the [virtuous] is a tree of life.
—Proverbs 11:30

Virtue is to the soul what health is to the body.
—François de la Rochefoucauld

Virtue is the most pleasing and valuable possession in the world.
—Plutarch

Virtue is a habit of the mind consistent with nature and moderation and reason.
—Cicero

Virtue is a habit that disposes one to do good. It allows a person not only to perform good acts but, by repetition, it allows the habit to become part of his or her nature.

Human virtues are habitual dispositions of the intellect, memory, and will that direct our actions according to faith and reason. These virtues, also called moral virtues, are acquired by education and perseverance, and elevated by divine grace. The moral virtues are given various names in the Scriptures and by spiritual writers, but these virtues are basically four in number: prudence, justice, fortitude, and temperance. They are also called the cardinal virtues because all the other human virtues can be grouped around them.

Prudence is the moral virtue that guides our practical reason to choose what is good in every situation and to select the best means of attaining it. Saint Thomas Aquinas describes prudence as right reason in action. Prudence guides the judgment of our conscience. The prudent person determines and directs his or her actions according to this judgment.

Justice is the moral virtue that prompts one to give God and neighbors that which they deserve. We offer praise, honor, glory, and thanksgiving to God just because God is God. We offer justice to others by respecting their rights and by promoting harmony and equality with regard to others and the common good.

Fortitude is the moral virtue that provides courage in the times of temptations, trials, and obstacles in our moral life. It also enables one to conquer fear, even the fear of death, and to face trials and persecution.

Temperance is the moral virtue that helps to moderate our attraction to pleasure and to give some balance in the use of created goods. In the past this virtue was primarily associated with excessive drinking. But it also reminds us that we can overindulge in most anything: golf, fishing, clothes, beauty, our pets. A temperate person directs his or her appetites toward what is good and maintains a healthy attitude in the use of the things of creation.

Prayer

God, for your honor and glory, for better relations with others, and for self-respect, grant me an increase in the virtues of prudence, justice, fortitude, and temperance. Amen.

Works of Mercy

. . . We do pray for mercy,
And that same prayer doth teach us all to render
The deeds of mercy.
                                    —William Shakespeare

Blessed are the merciful:
they shall have mercy shown them.
                                    —Matthew 5:7

Being all fashioned of the self-same dust,
Let us be merciful as well as just.
                                    —Henry Wadsworth Longfellow

Let faithful love and constancy never leave you;
tie them round your neck,
write them on the tablet of your heart.
                                    —Proverbs 3:3

Each of us has at one time or another performed some act of kindness and compassion. Not many people can walk away from another in need, whether it is a relative, a friend, or a stranger. This inclination seems to be part of human nature.

These works of mercy are charitable actions that prompt us to aid others in their bodily and spiritual needs. Corporal works of mercy are feeding the hungry, giving shelter to the homeless, clothing the naked, visiting the sick and those in prison, and burying the dead.

The spiritual works of mercy include such acts as instructing the ignorant, counseling the doubtful, consoling the sorrowful, comforting the oppressed, forgiving others, and being patient when wronged.

We are not strangers to some of these actions. We have performed all or some of them ourselves, and we see them taking place every day. We marvel at the good that is done through such organizations as the Red Cross, the Salvation Army, the Catholic Worker, UNICEF, the Mercy Ship, Catholic Charities, and the United Way, to mention a few. You are a part of the good deeds of these societies if you are or have been a member or have donated your time and talents to further their works of mercy.

Prayer

I pray for all those organizations engaged in assisting the oppressed and suffering in the world. May those of us who are more fortunate than others put into practice these words, "In so far as you did this to one of the least of these brothers of mine, you did it to me" (Matthew 25:40). Amen.